P9-CAJ-635

THE VEGETARIAN MICROWAVE COOKBOOK

THE VEGETARIAN MICROWAVE COOKBOOK

INTRODUCED BY GAIL DUFF

Exeter Books

NEW YORK

Microwave consultant: *Jennie Shapter*
Production: *Richard Churchill*

© Marshall Cavendish Limited 1986

First published in USA 1986 by Exeter Books
Distributed by Bookthrift
Exeter is a trademark of Bookthrift Marketing, Inc.
Bookthrift is a registered trademark of
Bookthrift Marketing
New York, New York

ALL RIGHTS RESERVED

ISBN 0-671-08211-6
D. L. TO:1028-1986
Phototypeset by Quadraset Ltd, Midsomer Norton, Avon.
Printed and bound in Spain by Artes Graficas Toledo S.A.

CONTENTS

INTRODUCTION

With a microwave oven you can cook fresh foods in minutes, thaw and reheat frozen ones with ease and save time and effort on numerous small but necessary parts of food preparation. Combine microwave with vegetarian cookery and you have the perfect team for wholesome meals cooked in minutes.

Vegetarian soups, appetizers, main dishes and accompaniments can be cooked to perfection in your microwave oven, and there will always be time to make a delicious dessert to round off the meal. Baking times for cakes, breads and cookies are also significantly cut when using a microwave oven. Such advantages will encourage you not only to cook more of your favorite dishes, but also to try new ones.

Most vegetarian ingredients can be cooked successfully in a microwave oven and many retain more nutrients than when cooked conventionally.

VEGETABLES

When vegetables are cooked in a microwave oven, they require very little water, and some need no more than a knob of butter. As a result, more vitamins are retained than when conventional boiling methods are used, the colors remain bright and the texture crisp but tender.

Vegetables can be cooked in roasting bags or in microproof dishes and containers. Most are best covered with a lid or plastic wrap. Where the vegetables are finely chopped or if they are small, such as peas or fava beans, they will cook better in a fairly shallow, wide-based container. Do not add salt to any vegetable that is to be cooked in a microwave oven as this may cause it to toughen. You will find that more natural flavors are retained when microwave cooking than when vegetables are cooked by conventional methods and so salt may not be necessary.

If liked, before cooking vegetables, sprinkle with herbs and/or dot with a knob of butter.

Beans, Fava: Add ⅔ cup water to every 2 lb unhulled weight of beans. Microwave at 100% (High) for 10 minutes, stirring after 5 minutes.

Beans, Green: Add stock or water to half cover. Cover; microwave at 100% (High) for 15 minutes.

Beans, English runner (snake): Slice. Add 1 tablespoon water per 1 lb beans. Cover and microwave at 100% (High) for 12–15 minutes.

Brussels Sprouts: Add ⅔ cup water per 1 lb. Cover and microwave at 100% (High) for 15 minutes.

Cabbage: Shred. Add ⅓ cup water per medium cabbage. Cover and microwave at 100% (High) for 10 minutes, stirring after 5 minutes.

Calabrese (Italian sprouting broccoli): Trim the heads and make sure they are even-size. Cut large ones lengthwise in two. Add ⅔ cup water per 1 lb. Cover and microwave at 100% (High) for 15 minutes.

Carrots: Slice or dice. Add ⅔ cup water per 1 lb. Cover and microwave at 100% (High) for 15 minutes.

Cauliflower: Break into small flowerets. Add ⅔ cup stock or water per medium cauliflower. Cover and microwave at 100% (High) for 20 minutes, stirring after 10 minutes.

Celery: Chop or cut into short lengths. Add ¾ cup stock or water per head of celery. Cover and microwave at 100% (High) for 12 minutes.

Eggplants: Cut in ½-inch slices and brush with oil. Arrange in a single layer on a flat plate, leave them uncovered and then microwave at 100% (High) for 3 minutes.

Leeks: Cut in short lengths if thin, or in ½ inch thick slices. Add ¼ cup stock or water per 1 lb. Cover and microwave at 100% (High) for 8–10 minutes.

Peas: Add ⅔ cup stock or water per 2 lb unhulled weight. Cover and microwave at 100% (High) for 10 minutes, stirring after 5 minutes. For small quantities (up to ½ lb) of young peas, add butter, cover and cook until tender.

Potatoes: In their skins, scrub and prick on all sides with a fork. Cooking time at 100% (High) depends on size and number of potatoes. Four medium potatoes take about 15 minutes. Or cook potatoes sliced or diced with 2 cups stock or water per 1½ lb. Cover and microwave at 100% (High) for 30 minutes.

Rutabaga: Dice. Add ⅔ cup stock or water per 1 lb. Cover and microwave at 100% (High) for 15–20 minutes.

Turnips: As for Rutabaga.

Zucchini: Slice. Add ⅓ cup stock or water per 1 lb. Cover and microwave at 100% (High) for 12 minutes.

EGGS

Eggs are as versatile in microwave cookery as they are when cooked in conventional ways. The only method not suitable for cooking eggs in a micro-wave is boiling, as cooking in the shell causes eggs to explode. Eggs should always be slightly under-cooked at the end of the cooking time as they will continue to cook by themselves for a few minutes; so always let them stand before serving. Another tip, remember to pierce the yolks with a cocktail pick or fine skewer when baking them whole.

CHEESE

Many main dishes containing cheese can be cooked in a microwave oven. Chese fondues can be made successfully, and cheese can also be mixed with a little milk or beer and melted to be spooned over toast for a perfect Welsh rarebit. Dishes topped with grated cheese can be microwaved for just a few minutes to heat the food and melt the cheese.

NUTS

Nut meals are becoming more popular and are a good source of protein for vegetarians. Many nut dishes can be cooked in a microwave oven; nut roasts are particularly successful and make a popular family Sunday lunch.

You can also use your microwave oven to skin and toast nuts before using them. To skin hazelnuts, spread about 3 tablespoons on a flat plate and microwave at 100% (High) for 2–2½ minutes, uncovered, giving the dish a gentle shake two or three times. Place the hazelnuts in a clean cloth and rub thoroughly to remove the skins. To toast almonds for decoration or garnish, spread about ¾ cup on a flat dish and microwave at 100% (High) for 5–7 minutes, rearranging several times, until the required color is achieved.

To test that vegetables are cooked, uncover and pierce with a fork

LEGUMES

The best way to use the microwave oven for cooking legumes is to prepare dishes using canned or precooked legumes which just need heating through. This is because the skins of dried peas or beans stay tough during the microwaving process and subsequently burst. Exceptions to this are those lentils which can be cooked straight from the package and split lentils which, because they are not totally encased in skin, do not burst.

RICE

Rice is an important vegetarian ingredient that cooks well in a microwave oven. However, there is very little saving in the cooking time of either brown or white rice compared with the conventional method of boiling it, but the resulting texture is very good.

To cook white rice, put a measured amount into a bowl with 1 teaspoon salt and 1 tablespoon oil. Pour on 3 cups boiling water to every 1½ cups rice. Cover with plastic wrap or a lid and microwave at 100% (High) for 10 minutes. Let the rice stand for 10 minutes before serving. For extra flavor, stock can be used in place of water.

Brown rice should be cooked in the same way as white rice, allowing 20 minutes cooking time and 15 minutes standing time.

PASTA

Both white and wholewheat pasta can be cooked in a microwave oven and the cooking time for each is the same. Put enough boiling water to cover the pasta into a large bowl with a little salt and 1 tablespoon oil. Add the pasta, bending long strips of spaghetti or lasagne to fit. Cover with plastic wrap or a lid and microwave at 100% (High) for 12 minutes. Leave the pasta in the water for 5 minutes before draining and using it.

BAKING

Pies, cakes, breads and biscuits can all be made with ease, speed and success.

Basic pie dough is the best dough for microwave cooking. Always make single crust pies because with double crust pies, the filling will tend to cook before the crust. To make open-faced pies and quiches, bake the unfilled pie shell first. Line a suitable pie dish with the dough and cover the pie with a double layer of absorbent kitchen paper. Microwave at 100% (High) for 4 minutes. Remove the paper and microwave for a further 1–2 minutes, depending on the size of the dish.

Microwave-cooked bread has a superb, moist texture. Bread made with white flour can be made to look attractive if brushed with beaten egg and sprinkled with cracked wheat or poppy seeds before baking. If wished, you can also finish the bread quickly under the browning element or the broiler of a conventional stove. Wholewheat flour will provide a better appearance.

Cakes cook very quickly in a microwave oven and therefore slightly less leavening agent is used since there is insufficient time for its taste to be cooked out.

Cakes cooked in a microwave oven look underdone when their cooking time is up, but they will firm during the standing time. Chocolate, spice and fruit cakes, plus those made with wholewheat flour and brown sugar, look fine; however, a plain layer cake can look rather pale and uncooked. To improve the color and its appearance, frost the cake or use toppings such as chopped nuts, coconut or a sprinkling of confectioners' sugar.

A shelf extends the available cooking space in this particular model

MICROWAVE KNOW-HOW

There are many different types of microwave ovens available, from the very simple to those with electronic touch pads and built-in browning elements and fan heaters. The most essential controls to look for on a microwave oven are the High, Medium, Low and Defrost settings. To ensure that the microwaves within the oven are evenly distributed, some ovens have an integral turntable which operates automatically when the oven is turned on. Others have what are called stirrer blades which move the microwaves around in the oven.

Microwave ovens are extremely safe, although they should be checked regularly for leakage. All doors are electrically sealed and the power automatically switches off as soon as the door is opened.

COOKWARE

Metal containers should usually be avoided in the microwave oven, although some of the latest models do permit limited use of metal. Avoid, too, china or glass with metal decorations, glassware made from lead crystal or earthenware with metal glazes. Metal reflects microwaves, preventing them from penetrating food and also possibly damaging the oven.

When buying china or pottery, check that it is suitable for microwave cookery. If you use glass, make sure that it is fairly thick, otherwise the temperature of the food could cause it to break.

Many kitchen stores now sell special microproof plastic containers in varying shapes and sizes. Plastic-coated or non-coated paper dinnerware is suitable, except when using the browner. So are roasting bags, but do not use metal twist-ties.

Food can be cooked 'en papillote' in waxed paper or baking parchment.

Wherever possible, use containers with rounded edges. Sharp corners attract the heat and, as a result, cause uneven cooking.

COOKING TECHNIQUES

Timing: The most important aspect of microwave cookery is timing. Unlike in a conventional oven, cooking times depend on how much food you want to cook at one time. The more food you put in, the longer the cooking time will be. This may cause problems when you are halving or doubling the ingredients in a recipe. Generally, if you double a recipe, you must increase the cooking time by between one-third and one-half again. Half the amount needs a cooking time of just over half the original time.

The temperature of your food will also alter the cooking time. Most recipes are designed for food at room temperature. If it has come directly from the refrigerator, increase the time slightly.

Preparing Food: Cooking times are also affected by the shape and size of food. Therefore, when you are preparing ingredients, make sure that they are similar in size and shape. For example, nut cutlets or other sorts of patties should be of an even thickness; and vegetables for a casserole should be cut in even-size cubes.

Arranging Food: Since microwaves penetrate from the outside to the center, food should ideally be placed around the outside of a dish, with a space in the center. When cooking chopped ingredients, arrange them in the dish in an even layer. Odd-shaped food should have the thicker parts pointing outward on the dish with the thinner parts toward the center.

Covering Food: If food is covered, the steam and moisture will be retained, so speeding up the cooking process and preventing the food from drying out. Many special microwave containers are supplied with a lid; if one is not available, use plastic wrap—seal it around the edges of the dish and then pierce with the point of a knife or a skewer.

Foods that you wish to keep dry, such as bread or dough, should be placed on a plate between sheets of absorbent kitchen paper.

Stirring and Rearranging: To ensure even cooking, most foods should be stirred or rearranged in the dish several times during the cooking time. If your microwave has no turntable or stirrer blade system, foods such as bread, nut roasts or cakes should be turned around at least once during the cooking time.

Standing Time: Most microwave recipes call for the food to be allowed to stand for a given time after cooking. This is important since foods continue to cook on their own after they have been removed from the oven. They may look slightly underdone at the beginning of the standing time, but when this time is up they should be cooked to perfection. Wait until standing time is complete before deciding whether the dish needs more time to cook.

SOUPS

Tasty soups can be made in the microwave in minutes using an endless variety of vegetables, herbs and spices. Whether it is hearty soups for cold winter days or chilled ones for hot summer days, cooking them in the microwave retains all the natural flavor of the ingredients.

The short cooking time ensures that added vegetable pieces keep their shape and crunchy texture. Cooking soups in the microwave also eliminates the danger of creamy soups burning in the bottom of a saucepan and ruining the flavor.

It is important to cook soups in a large casserole, allowing plenty of room for the liquid to boil without spilling over the edge. Although the microwave cooks quickly, it takes quite a long time to boil large quantities of liquid, so it is best to use hot stock.

Clear Turnip Soup (see page 16)

Zucchini Soup

COOKING	INGREDIENTS
14 mins	1 onion, chopped
	1 garlic clove, crushed
SETTING	1 tablespoon margarine or butter
	4 cups sliced zucchini
High	2 sprigs thyme or marjoram, or
STANDING	½ teaspoon dried herbs
	5 cups hot vegetable stock
None	few drops lemon juice
	salt and pepper
	¼ cup dairy sour cream, for garnish (optional)
	crusty bread, to serve
	Serves 4

1. Place the onion, garlic and margarine in a 2½-quart casserole and microwave at 100% (High) for 2 minutes. Add the zucchini, the herbs and the hot stock.
2. Cover with the lid and microwave at 100% (High) for 10 minutes, or until zucchini are tender.
3. Discard the fresh herbs, if used, let the soup cool slightly, then purée in a blender or food processor.
4. Return to the rinsed-out casserole, add the lemon juice and season with salt and pepper to taste, then cover and microwave at 100% (High) for 2 minutes to reheat.
5. Divide the soup among individual soup bowls, top with a spoonful of sour cream, if wished, and serve with crusty bread.

Clear Turnip Soup

COOKING	INGREDIENTS
9 mins	1 lb baby turnips, sliced and cut in small matchstick strips
SETTING	2 tablespoons margarine or butter
	2 garlic cloves, crushed
High	1 teaspoon Savita
STANDING	2 cups croûtons
	1 cup grated Gruyère cheese
None	chopped fresh parsley
	Serves 4

1. Place the turnips in a 2-quart casserole with 1 quart boiling water. Cover with the lid and microwave at 100% (High) for 2 minutes.
2. Drain well, reserving all the cooking liquor.
3. Place the margarine in a 2-quart casserole and then microwave at 100% (High) for 1 minute or until it foams.
4. Add the garlic and turnip sticks, stir and microwave at 100% (High) for 4 minutes. Stir twice.
5. Dissolve the Savita in the reserved cooking juices and add to the turnips. Season with salt and pepper to taste, cover with the lid and microwave at 100% (High) for 2 minutes.
6. Divide the croûtons among four soup bowls, pour the soup into the bowls and scatter with cheese. Sprinkle with parsley and serve.

Lentil Soup

COOKING	INGREDIENTS
27 mins	1½ cups red, green or brown lentils
	6¼ cups boiling vegetable stock
SETTING	1 onion, diced
High/	2 garlic cloves, crushed
Medium-High	1 green pepper, seeded and sliced
STANDING	1 teaspoon ground cumin
	juice of 1 lemon
None	salt and pepper
	fried onion rings, to serve
	Serves 6

1. Place the lentils in a 2½-quart casserole. Add the boiling stock, onion, garlic and green pepper. Cover with the lid and microwave at 100% (High) for 10 minutes.
2. Reduce to 70% (Medium-High) for 12 minutes or until the lentils have softened.
3. Let cool slightly, then purée half the contents of the dish in a blender or a food processor until smooth. If wished, purée the entire contents for a smoother soup.
4. Add the cumin, lemon juice and season with salt and pepper to taste. Stir well, cover and microwave at 100% (High) for 5 minutes.
5. Divide the soup among individual soup bowls and top each with a portion of fried onion rings.

Minestrone Soup

Minestrone Soup

COOKING	INGREDIENTS
16 mins	2 tablespoons olive oil
	1 red onion, chopped
SETTING	1 garlic clove, minced
	1 small leek, sliced
High/Medium	4 cups hot vegetable stock
	1 carrot, sliced
STANDING	2 celery stalks, sliced
	4 tablespoons tomato paste
None	1/4 small cabbage, shredded
	1/4 cup dried haricot beans, soaked overnight and cooked
	1/3 cup miniature pasta shapes or broken spaghetti
	salt and pepper
	2 tablespoons freshly grated Parmesan cheese
	2 tablespoons chopped fresh parsley
	grated Parmesan cheese, to serve
	Serves 4–6

1. Place the oil, the chopped onion, the minced garlic and the sliced leek in a 2½-quart casserole and set the microwave oven at 100% (High). Cook the vegetables for 3 minutes until they are tender.

2. Add the hot vegetable stock, the sliced carrot and celery. Cover the ingredients with the lid and microwave at 100% (High) for 5 minutes.

3. Stir in the tomato paste and cabbage, then cover again and microwave at 100% (High) for 3 minutes.

4. Add the cooked beans and pasta, cover and microwave at 100% (High) for 5–6 minutes, or until the pasta is cooked.

5. Season with salt and pepper to taste and then add the Parmesan cheese and the chopped parsley to the mixture and stir it in.

6. To serve, transfer the Minestone Soup to a large tureen (or divide among individual soup bowls), and pass the extra grated Parmesan cheese separately.

Chilled Tomato Soup

COOKING	INGREDIENTS
15½ mins	*2 lb tomatoes*
	2 tablespoons margarine or butter
SETTING	*2 onions, minced*
	2 carrots, finely chopped
High	*pinch of cayenne*
STANDING	*1 teaspoon dried basil*
	salt and pepper
None	*1 cup plain yogurt*
	¼ cup heavy cream
	2 tablespoons finely chopped fresh parsley, for garnish
	Serves 4

1. Cover the tomatoes with boiling water for 1 minute, then drain, peel and chop.
2. Place the margarine in a 2½-quart casserole and microwave at 100% (High) for 30 seconds to melt. Stir in the onions, carrots and cayenne.
3. Cover with the lid and microwave at 100% (High) for 5 minutes, stirring twice.
4. Add the chopped tomatoes and basil. Cover and microwave at 100% (High) for 10 minutes, or until the tomatoes are reduced to a purée. Stir them twice.
5. Let cool slightly, then purée in a blender or food processor until smooth. Return to the rinsed-out casserole, pouring it through a strainer. Season with salt and pepper to taste.

6. Let cool, then stir in the yogurt. Cover and chill for 2 hours.
7. Divide the soup among individual soup bowls and swirl 1 tablespoon heavy cream into each portion. Garnish with the finely chopped fresh parsley and then serve.

Chilled Tomato Soup

White and Orange Soup

COOKING	INGREDIENTS
10½ mins	*2 tablespoons margarine or butter*
	2 baby turnips, cut in matchstick strips
SETTING	*5 baby carrots, cut in matchstick strips*
	4 cups hot vegetable stock
High	*4 scallions, cut in thin strips*
STANDING	*1 tablespoon ground coriander or finely chopped fresh parsley*
None	*salt and pepper*
	toast or rolls, to serve
	Serves 6

1. Place the margarine in a 2-quart casserole and microwave at 100% (High) for 30 seconds to melt. Add the turnips and carrots, stir and cook at 100% (High) for 4 minutes. Stir after 2 minutes.
2. Add the hot stock and cover with the lid. Microwave at 100% (High) for 3 minutes.
3. Add the scallions and the coriander or the finely chopped parsley. Season with salt and pepper to taste. Cover again and microwave at 100% (High) for 3 minutes.
4. Divide the soup among individual soup bowls and serve with toast or rolls.

Creamy Vegetable Soup

COOKING	INGREDIENTS
16 mins	1 large onion, sliced
	8 scallions, chopped
SETTING	2 tablespoons margarine or butter
	4 cups hot vegetable stock
High	2 potatoes, chopped
STANDING	⅔ cup light cream
	4 tomatoes, peeled and chopped
None	½ cucumber, chopped
	salt and pepper
	FOR GARNISH:
	chopped fresh herbs
	lemon slices
	Serves 4

1. Place the onions and margarine in a 2½-quart casserole and microwave at 100% (High) for 3 minutes. Stir after 2 minutes.

2. Add the hot stock and potatoes, cover with the lid and microwave at 100% (High) for 10 minutes.

3. Let cool slightly, then purée in a blender or food processor. Return to the rinsed-out casserole, add the cream, tomatoes and cucumber and stir to mix.

4. Microwave at 100% (High) for 3–4 minutes to heat through, stirring 2–3 times. Season with salt and pepper to taste.

5. Divide the soup among individual soup bowls, garnish with the herbs and lemon slices and serve.

Chinese Leafy Soup

COOKING	INGREDIENTS
10 mins	1 bunch scallions
	4 cups boiling vegetable stock
SETTING	1 teaspoon grated fresh gingerroot
	2 teaspoons lemon juice
High	2 teaspoons soy sauce
STANDING	salt and pepper
	2 oz Chinese egg noodles
4 mins	2–3 lettuce leaves, finely shredded
	½ bunch watercress, chopped
	Serves 4

1. Finely shred the scallions diagonally, including the green tops.

2. Place the stock, two-thirds of the scallions, ginger, lemon juice and soy sauce in a 2½-quart casserole. Season with salt and pepper to taste. Cover and microwave at 100% (High) for 3 minutes.

3. Place the noodles in a large deep bowl with 5 cups boiling water. Cover with pierced plastic wrap and microwave at 100% (High) for 4 minutes. Let stand for 4 minutes, then drain.

4. Add the lettuce and watercress to the stock, cover and then microwave at 100% (High) for 3–4 minutes.

5. Divide the noodles among individual soup bowls, pour the soup on top, garnish with remaining scallions and serve.

Chinese Leafy Soup

Pea Soup with Cheese Wedges

Pea Soup with Cheese Wedges

COOKING	INGREDIENTS
9 mins	*1 tablespoon margarine*
	3 scallions, chopped
SETTING	*1½ cans (16 oz size) sweet peas*
	2½ cups hot vegetable stock
High	*1 teaspoon chopped fresh mint*
STANDING	*3 tablespoons instant potato mix*
	1 teaspoon lemon juice
None	*3 tablespoons light cream*
	salt and pepper
	CHEESE WEDGES:
	½ cup grated Cheddar cheese
	1 tablespoon light cream
	½ teaspoon prepared mustard
	salt and pepper
	4 small thick slices wholewheat toast
	TO SERVE:
	2 tablespoons chopped fresh parsley
	¼ cup grated Cheddar cheese
	Serves 4

1. Place the margarine in a 2-quart casserole with the scallions and then microwave the ingredients at 100% (High) for 2 minutes.

2. Purée the peas with their liquid and the scallions in a blender or food processor, then strain into the casserole.

3. Add the hot stock and mint. Cover and microwave at 100% (High) for 5 minutes, or until boiling.

4. Sprinkle in the potato mix and beat well using a hand-held electric mixer. Microwave at 100% (High) for 1–2 minutes, or until thick, stirring 2–3 times.

5. Stir in the lemon juice and cream. Season with salt and pepper to taste.

6. Mix the cheese for the wedges with the cream and mustard, then season with salt and pepper to taste. Spread over the toast.

7. Place the toast on a large plate lined with absorbent kitchen paper and microwave at 100% (High) for 1 minute. Rearrange after 30 seconds. If wished brown under a preheated broiler or microwave browning element. Cut in small squares.

8. Divide the soup among individual soup bowls. Top each portion with a cheese wedge and sprinkle with parsley and cheese. Serve with the remaining cheese wedges passed separately.

Bean and Rice Soup

COOKING	INGREDIENTS
23 mins	1 onion, minced
	2 garlic cloves, minced
SETTING	1 carrot, finely chopped
	2 celery stalks, finely chopped
High	1 tablespoon vegetable oil
STANDING	1 can (16 oz) tomatoes
	2½ cups hot vegetable stock
None	1 can (16 oz) borlotti or red kidney beans, drained and rinsed
	½ cup long-grain rice
	1 teaspoon dried basil
	2 tablespoons minced fresh parsley
	pinch of granulated sugar
	salt and pepper
	Serves 4

1. Place the onion, garlic, carrot, celery and oil in a 2½-quart casserole and microwave at 100% (High) for 4 minutes.
2. Add the tomatoes with their juice and the hot stock. Stir well, then cover with the lid and microwave at 100% (High) for 7 minutes.
3. Let cool slightly, then purée in a blender until smooth. Return to the rinsed-out casserole.
4. Add the rice, basil, parsley and sugar. Season to taste. Replace the lid and microwave at 100% (High) for 10 minutes. Stir after 7 minutes. Add the beans and microwave at 100% (High) for 2 minutes.
5. Serve the soup in individual soup bowls.

Watercress Soup

COOKING	INGREDIENTS
17 mins	2 bunches watercress, stems trimmed
	1 large onion, chopped
SETTING	3 tablespoons margarine or butter
	1 cup chopped potatoes
High	2½ cups hot vegetable stock
STANDING	salt and pepper
	⅔ cup light cream
None	⅞ cup milk
	¼ cup light cream, for garnish
	Serves 4

1. Place the watercress, onion and margarine in a large bowl. Cover with pierced plastic wrap and microwave at 100% (High) for 3 minutes, stirring after 2 minutes.
2. Add the potato and hot stock. Cover again and microwave at 100% (High) for 10 minutes, stirring twice.
3. Let cool slightly, then purée in a blender or food processor until smooth. Season the mixture to taste with salt and pepper.
4. Return to the rinsed-out bowl, cover with pierced plastic wrap and microwave at 100% (High) for 2 minutes.
5. Stir in the cream and milk and microwave at 100% (High) for 2 minutes.
6. Divide among individual soup bowls, garnish with swirls of cream and serve.

Artichoke Soup

COOKING	INGREDIENTS
20 mins	2 onions, chopped
	1 tablespoon margarine or butter
SETTING	2 lb Jerusalem artichokes, peeled and sliced
High	2 cups hot vegetable stock
STANDING	2½ cups milk
	salt and pepper
None	⅓ cup heavy double cream
	chopped fresh parsley, for garnish
	croûtons, to serve
	Serves 6

1. Place the onion and margarine in a 2½-quart casserole and microwave at 100% (High) for 2 minutes.
2. Add the artichokes and hot stock. Cover and microwave at 100% (High) for 15 minutes, or until the artichokes are soft.
3. Cool slightly, then purée in a blender or food processor. Return to the rinsed-out casserole.
4. Add the milk and season with salt and pepper to taste. Cover and microwave at 100% (High) for 3 minutes, or until hot.
5. Divide the soup among individual soup bowls, swirl a spoonful of cream into each bowl and sprinkle with parsley. Serve with croûtons.

Chunky Vegetable Soup

COOKING	INGREDIENTS
14 mins	5 cups hot vegetable stock
	1 head celery, sliced
SETTING	4 large carrots, sliced
	1 tablespoon cornstarch
High	1 cup small button mushrooms, wiped
STANDING	½ cup light cream
	salt and pepper
None	chopped fresh parsley, for garnish
	Serves 4

1. Place the hot stock, celery and carrots in a 2½-quart casserole. Cover with the lid and microwave at 100% (High) for 10 minutes or until the vegetables are just tender.
2. Mix the cornstarch to a paste with 2 tablespoons water and stir into the soup. Cover again and microwave at 100% (High) for 2 minutes, or until thick, stirring twice.
3. Add the mushrooms, cover and microwave at 100% (High) for 2 minutes. Stir in the cream and then season the mushroom soup with salt and pepper to taste.
4. Divide the soup among individual soup bowls, sprinkle with chopped parsley and serve.

Creamy Scallion Soup

COOKING	INGREDIENTS
7 mins	1 bunch scallions, trimmed and sliced
	2 tablespoons butter
SETTING	1 tablespoon dry mustard
	1 tablespoon all-purpose flour
High	2½ cups hot vegetable stock
STANDING	2 tablespoons mild wholegrain mustard
	½ teaspoon lemon juice
None	2 egg yolks
	1¼ cups light cream
	salt and pepper
	Serves 4

1. Reserve 4 tablespoons scallion tops. Place the butter and remaining scallions in a 2-quart casserole; microwave at 100% (High) for 2 minutes.
2. Stir in the dry mustard and flour. Gradually stir in the hot stock, wholegrain mustard and lemon juice. Microwave at 100% (High) for 4–5 minutes, or until thick, stirring 2–3 times.
3. Beat the egg yolks and cream together and stir into the soup. Microwave at 100% (High) for 1–1½ minutes, or until thick. Do not let the soup boil.
4. Season to taste, then serve sprinkled with the reserved scallion tops.

Chunky Vegetable Soup

Vichyssoise

COOKING	INGREDIENTS
20 mins	4 potatoes, thinly sliced
	4 vegetable bouillon cubes
SETTING	¼ cup butter or margarine
	1¼ cups light cream
High	2 leeks, trimmed and thinly sliced
STANDING	1 onion, minced
	2½ cups milk
None	pepper and ¼ teaspoon salt
	chopped chives, for garnish
	Serves 4–6

Vichyssoise

1. Place the potatoes and crumbled bouillon cubes in a 2½-quart casserole dish. Add ½ cup hot water, stir and cover. Microwave at 100% (High) for 12 minutes, or until tender, stirring twice.
2. Add half the butter and ⅔ cup cream to the potatoes and set the casserole aside.
3. Combine the leeks, onion and remaining butter in a 2-quart casserole. Cover with the lid and microwave at 100% (High) for 8–10 minutes, or until tender, stirring twice.

4. Cool slightly, then purée the onion mix with the potato mix and remaining cream in a blender.
5. Return to the rinsed-out 2½-quart casserole. Add the milk, pepper and salt.
6. To serve hot, cover the soup and microwave at 100% (High) for 2 minutes. To serve cold, chill for 2 hours before serving.
7. Divide the soup among individual soup bowls, garnish with chopped chives and serve.

Asparagus Soup

COOKING	INGREDIENTS
19 mins	1 lb asparagus, trimmed
	5 large scallions
SETTING	1 onion, chopped
	2 tablespoons margarine or butter
High	2½ cups hot vegetable stock
STANDING	½ cup all-purpose flour
	1½ cups milk
None	salt and pepper
	¼ cup heavy cream
	Serves 4

1. Cut the asparagus in 1-inch lengths. Set the tips aside. Chop the green parts of the scallions, then slice the white bulbs in rings and reserve.
2. Place the chopped green parts of the scallions in a 2½-quart casserole. Add the asparagus stalks, onion, margarine and half the hot stock. Cover

tightly and microwave at 100% (High) for 10 minutes. Stir after 5 minutes.
3. Gradually mix the remaining stock with the flour, stirring constantly. Stir in a little hot soup, then pour the mixture back into the casserole.
4. Microwave at 100% (High) for 2–3 minutes or until thick, stirring 2–3 times.
5. Let the soup cool slightly, then purée in a blender. Stir in the milk and seasoning to taste.
6. Place the reserved asparagus tips in a small bowl with ¼ cup water. Cover with pierced plastic wrap and microwave at 100% (High) for 4 minutes. Add the scallion rings, cover and microwave at 100% (High) for 1 minute. Drain.
7. Reheat the soup, covered, at 100% (High) for 2–3 minutes, then stir in the cream.
8. Pour the soup into soup bowls, garnish each with asparagus tips and scallion rings and serve.

SNACKS

When it comes to preparing fast food for snacks, the microwave is invaluable. It is all too easy to turn to convenience meals when time is short, but with the microwave fast healthy food is simple.

This chapter has snacks to suit all appetites, from Lentil Filled Pitas and Rice Stuffed Tomatoes to Avocado and Apple Snack and Lemony Asparagus, both of which could be served as appetizers at the smartest dinner party.

Eggs and cheese play an important part in a vegetarian diet. They are extremely versatile and can be used to make all kinds of nourishing snacks and appetizers. As both are sensitive to heat, they cook very quickly and require careful timing to make sure that they do not become overcooked.

Paprika Eggs with Yogurt (see page 29)

Savory Onion and Monterey Jack

COOKING	INGREDIENTS
11 mins	4 large onions, thickly sliced
	½ cup milk
SETTING	salt and pepper
	1½ cups grated Monterey Jack cheese
High	2 tablespoons butter
STANDING	6 slices buttered toast, crusts removed and cut in triangles, to serve
10 mins	**Serves 6**

1. Put the onions in a 2-quart bowl with ⅓ cup water. Cover with pierced plastic wrap and microwave at 100% (High) for 6 minutes, or until the onions are soft. Drain.

2. Add the milk, stir and season with salt and pepper. Microwave at 100% (High) for 3 minutes.

3. Cover the onion mixture with a thick layer of cheese and dot with the butter. Cover with pierced plastic wrap and let stand for 10 minutes.

4. Stir the cheese and onion mixture once, then microwave, uncovered, at 100% (High) for 2 minutes, stirring twice. Serve with hot buttered toast.

Avocado and Apple Snack

COOKING	INGREDIENTS
4 mins	2 tablespoons margarine
	¼ cup all-purpose flour
SETTING	1¼ cups milk
	¾ cup shredded sharp Cheddar cheese
High	2 teaspoons Dijon mustard
STANDING	salt and pepper
	2 ripe avocados
None	4 crisp dessert apples
	1 tablespoon lemon juice
	½ cup soft brown bread crumbs
	Serves 4

1. Place the margarine in a 3-cup bowl and microwave at 100% (High) for 30 seconds to melt.

Stir in the flour then gradually add the milk, stirring continuously.

2. Microwave at 100% (High) for 3–4 minutes, or until thick, stirring 2–3 times. Stir in ½ cup cheese and the mustard. Season to taste.

3. Pare the avocados, cut in half and remove the seeds. Cut lengthwise in thin slices.

4. Pare, quarter and core the apples. Cut in thin slices. Arrange the slices of avocado and apple in layers in 4 individual shallow gratin dishes. Sprinkle with lemon juice, to prevent discoloration.

5. Pour the sauce over the avocado and apple. Mix together the remaining cheese and the bread crumbs and sprinkle evenly over the top.

6. Place under a preheated broiler or microwave browning element for about 5 minutes until golden brown and bubbling.

Avocado and Apple Snack

Lentil Filled Pitas

Lentil Filled Pitas

COOKING	INGREDIENTS
25 mins	*3 tablespoons margarine or butter*
	1 onion, minced
SETTING	*1 cup thinly sliced button mushrooms*
	2 teaspoons ground cumin
High/Medium	*1⅓ cups split red lentils*
STANDING	*2 cups boiling vegetable stock*
	2 tablespoons lemon juice
None	*1 tablespoon chopped fresh parsley*
	salt and pepper
	4 white or brown pita breads
	4 tomatoes, thinly sliced
	2 inch length of cucumber, cubed
	½ cup crumbled goat's cheese
	shredded lettuce and black olives
	Serves 4

1. Place the margarine in a 2½-quart casserole. Add the minced onion and then microwave it at 100% (High) for 3 minutes.

2. Add ¾ cup mushrooms and cumin. Stir and microwave at 100% (High) for 2 minutes. Add the lentils and boiling stock. Stir, cover with a lid and microwave at 100% (High) for 4 minutes, or until the contents are boiling.

3. Reduce to 50% (Medium) for 15 minutes, or until the lentils are soft and the liquid has been absorbed. Stir occasionally.

4. Add the lemon juice and parsley. Season with salt and pepper to taste.

5. Dampen the pita breads by sprinkling them all over with a little cold water. Place on absorbent kitchen paper in the microwave oven and microwave the dampened pita breads at 100% (High) for 45–60 seconds.

6. Cut the pita breads in half horizontally, and ease open with a round-bladed knife. Divide the lentil mixture among the pita pockets. Top with the tomatoes, cucumber, cheese, lettuce, olives and the remaining mushrooms to serve.

Egg and Onion Bake

Egg and Onion Bake

COOKING	INGREDIENTS
38 mins	*4 eggs, lightly beaten*
	salt and pepper
SETTING	*2½ cups milk*
High/Low/ Medium	*¼ cup shredded sharp Cheddar cheese*
STANDING	*1 tablespoon margarine or butter*
	1 tablespoon vegetable oil
None	*2 large onions, minced*
	2 tablespoons chopped chervil
	SAUCE:
	2 tablespoons margarine or butter
	¼ cup all-purpose flour
	1¼ cups milk
	1 cup shredded Cheddar cheese
	Serves 4

1. Lightly grease a 1½-quart heatproof oval dish with margarine.

2. Place the eggs in a bowl, season with salt and pepper to taste and beat together.

3. Place the milk in a 3-cup liquid measure and microwave at 100% (High) for 4 minutes, or until almost boiling. Pour onto the eggs and beat to combine. Stir in the cheese.

4. Pour into the prepared dish and stand in a slightly larger shallow dish. Pour enough hot water into the outer dish to come 1 inch up the sides of the oval dish.

5. Microwave at 30% (Low) for 20 minutes, then 50% (Medium) for 6 minutes, or until the center of the custard is just set. Give the dish a quarter turn every 5 minutes.

6. Place the margarine, oil and onions in a 1½-quart bowl and microwave at 100% (High) for 4 minutes, stirring after 2 minutes. Next, stir in the chervil.

7. Make the sauce: Place the margarine in a 5-cup bowl and microwave at 100% (High) for 30 seconds to melt.

8. Stir in the flour, then gradually add the milk. Microwave at 100% (High) for 3–4 minutes, or until thick, stirring 2–3 times. Stir in half the cheese and season with salt and pepper to taste.

9. Spoon the onion mixture onto the egg mixture.

10. Spoon the sauce over the onions and sprinkle with the remaining cheese.

11. Place the dish under a preheated broiler or microwave browning element until the cheese is golden brown and bubbling. Serve immediately.

Paprika Eggs with Yogurt

COOKING	INGREDIENTS
8 mins	1¼ cups plain yogurt
	2 teaspoons cornstarch
SETTING	1½ tablespoons milk
	2 garlic cloves, crushed
High/Medium	salt and pepper
STANDING	4 large eggs
	1 tablespoon margarine or butter
2 mins	½ teaspoon mild paprika
	1 tablespoon chopped fresh parsley
	Serves 4

1. Place the yogurt in a 3-cup liquid measure jug and microwave at 100% (High) for 45 seconds. Stir after 30 seconds.
2. Mix the cornstarch and milk together and stir into the yogurt.
3. Microwave at 100% (High) for 2–2½ minutes, or until thick, stirring 3–4 times, in one direction.
4. Beat in the garlic and season with salt and pepper to taste. Divide among 4 ramekin dishes or custard cups. Top each with an egg. Prick the yolks with a cocktail pick, but be careful not to break them.
5. Cover each dish with plastic wrap, leaving one-fourth of the dish uncovered.
6. Place the dishes in a circle in the microwave oven and microwave at 50% (Medium) for 4½–5½ minutes or until the white is barely set. Re-arrange the dishes after 2 minutes. Let stand for 2 minutes.
7. Place the margarine in a small bowl and microwave at 100% (High) for 20 seconds to melt. Add the paprika to the melted margarine, mix and pour over the eggs.
8. Sprinkle with the chopped parsley and serve.

Cheesy Scramble

COOKING	INGREDIENTS
6 mins	½ cup chopped mushrooms
	2 tablespoons butter or margarine
SETTING	8 eggs
	¼ cup milk
High	¼ teaspoon dry mustard
STANDING	salt and pepper
	½ cup shredded Cheddar cheese
None	butter, for spreading
	4 thick slices of toast
	parsley sprigs, for garnish
	Serves 4

1. Place the mushrooms and 1 tablespoon butter in a small bowl and microwave at 100% (High) for 2 minutes.
2. Beat the eggs together with the milk and mustard. Season with salt and pepper. Place the remaining butter in a 5-cup bowl and microwave at 100% (High) for 20–30 seconds, to melt.
3. Pour in the egg mixture and microwave at 100% (High) for 3½–4 minutes until the eggs are just scrambled; stir 2–3 times. Add the cheese.

4. Butter the toast, then top each slice with mushrooms. Pile the cheesy scrambled egg on top, garnish with parsley sprigs and serve.

Cheesy Scramble

Grape Leaves with Rice and Walnuts

COOKING	INGREDIENTS
29 mins	2 tablespoons margarine or butter
	1 large onion, chopped
SETTING	1 garlic clove, chopped
	1 cup risotto rice
High	⅔ cup dry white wine
STANDING	1⅔ cups boiling vegetable stock
None	1 can (8 oz) grape leaves in brine, drained
	½ cup roughly chopped walnuts
	½ teaspoon ground coriander
	½ teaspoon ground cumin
	grated rind and juice of ½ lemon
	salt and pepper
	walnut halves, for garnish
	Serves 4

1. Place the margarine in a 2½-quart bowl and add the onion and garlic. Microwave at 100% (High) for 2 minutes. Add the rice, stir the ingredients and then microwave them at 100% (High) for 1 minute.

2. Add the wine and microwave at 100% (High) for 2 minutes. Add the boiling stock, cover with pierced plastic wrap and microwave at 100% (High) for 12 minutes or until the liquid is absorbed.

3. Place the grape leaves in a 2½-quart bowl containing 5 cups boiling salted water. Microwave at 100% (High) for 2 minutes. Drain the leaves on absorbent kitchen paper.

4. Spoon the rice mixture into a bowl and add the walnuts, spices and lemon rind. Season with salt and pepper to taste.

5. Spread 1 tablespoon of the filling over each grape leaf and wrap into packages. Pack closely together in layers in a lightly oiled microproof casserole. Pour over the lemon juice and just enough hot water to cover.

6. Cover with the casserole lid and microwave at 100% (High) for 10 minutes. Transfer to a serving dish with a wetted spoon. Garnish the rice-filled leaves with the walnut halves. This dish may be served either hot or cold.

Curried Nappa Cabbage

COOKING	INGREDIENTS
10 mins	3 tablespoons vegetable oil
	3 tablespoons light brown sugar
SETTING	¼ cup dry sherry
High/	1 tablespoon distilled white vinegar
Medium-High	3 tablespoons soy sauce
STANDING	1½ tablespoons mild curry powder
	salt
None	1 small onion, diced
	1 can (8 oz) bamboo shoots, drained and diced
	1½ cups bean sprouts
	¾ cup sliced mushrooms
	12 large leaves Nappa cabbage
	hot tomato sauce, to serve (optional)
	Serves 4–6

1. In a large bowl combine the oil, sugar, sherry, vinegar, soy sauce, curry powder and salt. Add the onion, bamboo shoots, bean sprouts and mushrooms. Stir into the mixture. Cover and let stand for 2–4 hours.

2. Blanch the cabbage leaves in a large bowl of boiling water at 100% (High) for 1 minute. Drain them well, leave them to cool then carefully separate the leaves.

3. Drain the marinated vegetables, reserve the liquid. Spread 1 tablespoon of the vegetables over each cabbage leaf and then wrap each one into a package.

4. Tie the parcels with strong cotton. Place in a shallow microproof dish and pour over the marinade. Cover with pierced plastic wrap and microwave the parcels at 70% (Medium-High) for 10–11 minutes.

5. Carefully remove the cotton from the parcels and serve them, with hot tomato sauce, handed separately, if wished.

Rice Stuffed Tomatoes

COOKING	INGREDIENTS
20 mins	6–8 large ripe tomatoes, about 3 oz each
SETTING	1 Bermuda onion, minced
High/ Medium-High	2 garlic cloves, chopped
	6 tablespoons chopped fresh parsley
STANDING	1 tablespoon chopped fresh mint
None	6–8 tablespoons cooked long-grain rice
	salt and pepper
	4 teaspoons grated Parmesan cheese
	⅓–½ cup olive oil
	TOMATO SAUCE:
	2 tablespoons butter
	1 carrot, diced
	1 onion, diced
	1 tablespoon all-purpose flour
	1 garlic clove, minced
	1 bay leaf
	¼ teaspoon dried thyme
	1 whole clove
	1 can (28 oz) tomatoes, drained
	salt and pepper
	Serves 3–4

1. For the sauce, place the butter in a 2-quart casserole, add the diced carrot and the diced onion and microwave at 100% (High) for 5 minutes, stirring 2–3 times.

2. Sprinkle in the flour, add the remaining sauce ingredients and mix them together well. Microwave them at 100% (High) for 8 minutes, stirring occasionally.

3. Cool slightly, then pour into a blender or food processor. Remove the bay leaf and clove then work until smooth.

4. Cut a thin slice from the top of each tomato and scoop out the seeds and pulp.

5. Combine the onion, garlic, parsley and mint in a bowl. Stir in the cooked rice and 6 tablespoons of the tomato sauce. Next, season with salt and pepper to taste.

6. Season the inside of the tomato shells with salt and pepper. Fill with the rice mixture. Top each with Parmesan cheese and 1 teaspoon olive oil. Place in a buttered gratin dish.

7. Microwave at 70% (Medium-High) for 4 minutes, rearranging after 2 minutes. Watch carefully in case the tomatoes overcook.

8. Pour a little sauce around the tomatoes and microwave at 100% (High) for 1 minute. Reheat the remaining sauce in a sauceboat at 100% (High) for 1½–2 minutes. Serve the tomatoes with the sauce passed separately.

Rice Stuffed Tomatoes

Saucy Cauliflower and Egg

COOKING	INGREDIENTS
10 mins	1 cauliflower, broken into flowerets
	salt and pepper
SETTING	2 hard-cooked eggs, shelled and quartered
High	SAUCE:
	2 tablespoons margarine or butter
STANDING	¼ cup all-purpose flour
None	1¼ cups hot vegetable stock
	1¼ cups dairy sour cream
	1 tablespoon chopped fresh parsley
	salt and pepper
	parsley or chervil sprigs, for garnish
	Serves 4

1. Place the cauliflower flowerets in a single layer in a shallow dish. Add ¼ cup water, cover with pierced plastic wrap and microwave at 100% (High) for 6–7 minutes.

2. Make the sauce: Place the margarine in a 1½-quart bowl and microwave at 100% (High) for 30 seconds, to melt.

3. Stir in the flour then gradually add the stock. Microwave at 100% (High) for 3–4 minutes, or until thick, stirring 2–3 times.

4. Add the sour cream and chopped parsley or chervil. Microwave at 100% (High) for 30 seconds. Season with salt and pepper to taste.

5. Drain the cauliflower and season. Add the eggs to the cauliflower. Pour the sauce over, garnish with parsley or chervil sprigs and serve.

Saucy Cauliflower and Egg

Cardamom Mushrooms

COOKING	INGREDIENTS
5 mins	3 tablespoons olive oil
	1 tablespoon lemon juice
SETTING	4 cups thinly sliced button mushrooms
	6 cardamom seeds, crushed
High	salt and pepper
STANDING	FOR GARNISH:
	coriander sprigs
None	lemon twists
	Serves 6

Cardamom Mushrooms

1. Mix the olive oil and lemon juice with 2 tablespoons water and place in a 2-quart serving dish. Add the mushrooms and cardamom seeds. Season with salt and pepper to taste.
2. Cover with pierced plastic wrap and microwave at 100% (High) for 5 minutes.
3. Remove from the microwave oven and let cool for about 2 hours.

4. Serve in a large dish or in individual bowls with the juices. Garnish with coriander and lemon twists and serve at room temperature.

Artichokes with Hollandaise Sauce

COOKING	INGREDIENTS
17 mins	4 globe artichokes
	1 teaspoon salt
SETTING	2 tablespoons lemon juice
High/ Medium-High	HOLLANDAISE SAUCE:
	⅓ cup white wine vinegar
STANDING	6 peppercorns
	1 bay leaf
None	3 egg yolks
	½ cup soft butter
	salt and pepper
	Serves 4

1. Place the artichokes in cold salted water for 30 minutes to remove any grit and insects.
2. Drain, then trim off the top leaves about a third of the way down. Cut off the stem.
3. Place in a large casserole, add 1 cup water, salt and lemon juice. Stir to dissolve the salt. Cover with pierced plastic wrap and microwave at 100% (High) for 14–15 minutes.

4. To test if cooked, try to pull a leaf from the artichoke. If it comes away freely the artichoke is cooked, if not, cover and microwave at 100% (High) for a few minutes. Drain upside down.
5. Place the vinegar, peppercorns and bay leaf in a 3-cup liquid measure and microwave at 100% (High) for 2 minutes, or until vinegar is reduced to 1¾ tablespoons.
6. Discard the peppercorns and bay leaf. Place in a food processor or blender with the egg yolks. Work for a few seconds until smooth.
7. Place the butter in a bowl and microwave at 100% (High) for 45–60 seconds until melted and bubbly. Blend the egg yolks at low speed, adding the butter in a slow and steady stream until the sauce thickens.
8. If necessary microwave at 70% (Medium-High) for 15–30 seconds, to thicken fully. Watch carefully as the sauce will curdle if overcooked.
9. Pour into a warmed sauceboat. Serve the artichokes with the sauce passed separately.

Avocados with Tomatoes

COOKING	INGREDIENTS
8 mins	4 tomatoes
	1 onion, minced
SETTING	1 garlic clove, crushed
	2 tablespoons butter or margarine
High	¼ teaspoon hot chili powder
STANDING	1½ cups fresh wholewheat bread crumbs
None	2 large avocados
	1½ tablespoons lemon juice
	salt and pepper
	¼ cup grated Parmesan cheese
	Serves 4

1. Using a small sharp knife, cut around the equators of two tomatoes in a zig-zag pattern. Prise the halves apart to make 4 waterlilies.

2. Scoop out the flesh from the centers and put it into a bowl. Skin and chop the remaining tomatoes and add to the bowl.

3. Put the onion, garlic and butter into a 1½-quart bowl and microwave at 100% (High) for 2 minutes. Add the chili powder and microwave at 100% (High) for 30 seconds.

4. Add the bread crumbs and chopped tomatoes to the onion mixture and reserve.

5. Halve the avocados and remove the seeds. Scoop out the flesh and place in a 1½-quart bowl. Brush the shells with a little lemon juice.

6. Mash the flesh with the remaining lemon juice and add to the onion mix. Season to taste. Use to fill both the avocado and tomato shells.

7. Arrange the stuffed avocados on a large plate with the pointed ends in and microwave at 100% (High) for 3 minutes.

8. Sprinkle the avocado stuffing with Parmesan cheese. Arrange stuffed tomatoes between the avocados and microwave at 100% (High) for 2–3 minutes, or until the tomatoes are hot but not slushy. Serve immediately.

Lemony Asparagus

COOKING	INGREDIENTS
11 mins	1 lb asparagus stalks, trimmed
	⅓ cup butter
SETTING	2 tablespoons lemon juice
	salt and pepper
High	lemon slices, for garnish
STANDING	**Serves 4**
5 mins	

1. Place the asparagus in a 12 × 8-inch dish with the stalks pointing in. Add ½ cup hot water and cover with pierced plastic wrap.

2. Microwave at 100% (High) for 10–11 minutes, or until tender. Rearrange the stalks and give the dish a half turn, halfway through the cooking time.

3. Let stand for 5 minutes, then drain.

4. Place the butter and lemon juice in a small bowl. Microwave at 100% (High) for 1–1½ minutes or until the butter has melted. Season with salt and pepper to taste. Stir.

5. Pour over the asparagus stalks, garnish with lemon slices and serve. Alternatively, pass the butter and lemon sauce separately.

Lemony Asparagus

Stuffed Eggplants

Stuffed Eggplants

COOKING	INGREDIENTS
27 mins	*2 eggplants*
	salt
SETTING	*2 tablespoons pignoli*
	1 tablespoon butter
High	*2 tablespoons vegetable oil*
STANDING	*TOPPING:*
	2 onions, chopped
None	*2 tablespoons olive oil*
	2 garlic cloves, crushed
	1 can (16 oz) tomatoes
	2 tablespoons golden raisins
	salt and pepper
	2 tablespoons chopped fresh parsley
	Serves 6

1. Cut the eggplants in ½ inch round slices. Sprinkle them with salt and leave to "sweat" in a colander for about 1 hour.

2. Place the pignoli and butter in a shallow dish and microwave at 100% (High) for 4–5 minutes or until lightly browned.

3. For the topping: Place the onions, oil and garlic in a 2-quart bowl and microwave at 100% (High) for 3 minutes. Add the tomatoes with half their juice and the golden raisins. Season to taste.

4. Microwave at 100% (High) for 10 minutes, or until the liquid is reduced, but the mixture is still moist. Stir in the parsley.

5. Rinse the salt off the eggplants and squeeze a few slices together between the palms of your hands to remove some of the juices.

6. Press them on absorbent kitchen paper, then arrange in one layer on a large serving platter. Sprinkle with oil, cover with pierced plastic wrap and microwave at 100% (High) for 10 minutes. Rearrange after 5 minutes.

7. Spread a little of the topping over each slice. Sprinkle pignoli on top and cool to room temperature before serving.

Cauliflower and Golden Raisin Salad

Cauliflower and Golden Raisin Salad

COOKING	INGREDIENTS
21 mins	*1 cauliflower, broken into flowerets*
	1 lb pearl onions
SETTING	*1 cup white wine*
	⅓ cup olive oil
High	*2 tablespoons wine vinegar*
STANDING	*3 tomatoes, peeled, seeded and chopped*
	3 tablespoons golden raisins
None	*1 teaspoon dark brown sugar*
	½ teaspoon dried thyme
	½ teaspoon ground coriander
	salt and pepper
	Serves 6

1. Place the cauliflower in a shallow dish in a single layer with 2 tablespoons water. Cover with pierced plastic wrap and microwave at 100% (High) for 4 minutes. Drain.

2. Place the onions in a shallow dish in a single layer with 3 tablespoons water. Cover with pierced plastic wrap and microwave at 100% (High) for 3 minutes. Drain.

3. Rinse both vegetables under cold running water to refresh. Drain the vegetables again.

4. Put the remaining ingredients in a 2-quart bowl with ½ cup water. Stir well to mix and microwave at 100% (High) for 5 minutes, stirring the ingredients twice.

5. Add the cauliflower and onions, cover with pierced plastic wrap and microwave at 100% (High) for 4 minutes, stirring occasionally.

6. Using a slotted spoon, transfer the vegetables to a serving dish. Microwave the sauce left in the bowl at 100% (High) for 5 minutes to reduce slightly. Pour over the vegetables and leave until cold. Serve at room temperature.

Vegetable Terrine

COOKING	INGREDIENTS
13 mins	¾ lb carrots, scraped
	¾ lb small zucchini, trimmed
SETTING	salt and pepper
	2 cups boiling vegetable stock
High	1 teaspoon Savita
STANDING	2 teaspoons agar-agar
	4 tablespoons mayonnaise
None	¼ cup heavy cream
	1 tablespoon tomato paste
	1 tablespoon chopped fresh parsley
	2 teaspoons lemon juice
	Serves 6–8

1. Thinly slice the carrots lengthwise, then cut them in ½-inch thick sticks. Repeat with the zucchini.

2. Place the carrots in a 2-quart bowl, add 3 tablespoons water, cover with pierced plastic wrap and microwave at 100% (High) for 8 minutes. Drain thoroughly and cool. Season with salt and pepper to taste.

3. Place the zucchini in a 2-quart bowl, add 2 tablespoons water, cover with pierced plastic wrap and microwave at 100% (High) for 5 minutes. Drain thoroughly and let cool. Season with salt and pepper to taste.

4. Arrange alternate strips of carrot and zucchini lengthwise over the base of a 9 × 5-inch loaf pan. Continue with alternate layers, in the same direction until all the vegetables are used.

5. Place the boiling stock in a liquid measure, mix in the Savita, then beat in the agar-agar.

6. Mix together the mayonnaise, cream, tomato paste, parsley and lemon juice. Season with salt and pepper to taste. Add to the stock and beat together. Work quickly as the agar may start to set.

7. Pour over the vegetables. Shake the pan gently to let the mixture flow between the vegetables. Bang sharply on the worktop to remove any air bubbles.

8. Cover and refrigerate until set. Run a knife around the top edge of the terrine, invert onto a serving dish and remove the pan. Serve sliced.

Vegetable Terrine

Greek Style Mushrooms

COOKING	INGREDIENTS
12 mins	3 tablespoons olive oil
	1 onion, minced
SETTING	1 tablespoon lemon juice
	1 garlic clove, crushed
High	2 sprigs thyme or ½ teaspoon dried thyme
STANDING	2 bay leaves
None	¾ lb tomatoes, peeled, seeded and chopped
	3 tablespoons chopped fresh parsley
	1½ lb very small button mushrooms
	Serves 6

1. Place the oil and onion in a 2-quart casserole. Microwave at 100% (High) for 2 minutes.

2. Add the lemon juice, garlic, thyme, bay leaves, tomatoes, half the parsley and 7 tablespoons water. Microwave at 100% (High) for 5 minutes, stirring occasionally.

3. Add the mushrooms, cover with the lid and microwave at 100% (High) for 5 minutes. Discard the thyme and bay leaves.

4. Transfer to a serving dish and sprinkle with the remaining parsley. The mushrooms may be served either cool or chilled.